AMERICAN REVOLUTION
INSPIRING STORIES FOR KIDS

A Collection of Memorable True Tales About Courage, Goodness, Rescue, and Civic Duty To Inspire Young Readers About Positive Lessons in The War of Independence

by

ENNIS JEMMY

Table of Contents

Introduction

The American Revolution is known as the process of liberation of the 13 American colonies from British rule, and from which the United States of America was formed with full sovereignty and endorsed by the Declaration of Independence. This confrontation between the freedom-seeking American colonists, known as "Patriots", and British soldiers lasted from 1775 to 1783. Although a good number of the colonists fought for freedom, almost a third of them supported the British monarchy, so we can assume that internal conflicts were very present during this period.

You must know that before the outbreak of the Revolution, a series of tense events occurred between the American colonists and members of the British Armed Forces. Two of these events were the Boston Massacre, which was an armed conflict that occurred in March 1770, and the Boston Tea Party which took place on December 16, 1773, where the colonists disguised as Mohawk Indians threw a shipload of tea into the ocean.

In addition, with the new government of King George III, Great Britain began to exercise greater control and impose high taxes to raise money for the protection of the British Empire during the French and Indian War.

Some laws were enacted to make these government changes possible, such as the Sugar Act in 1764 and a year later the Stamp Act, the latter being repealed because of the protests that were initiated and the resignation of the stamp agents who were called to work in the colonies. "No taxation without representation" became an iconic slogan in the wake of these imposed laws, as the colonists demanded a form of representation in the Parliament that they did not have at the time.

The people were enraged by the imposed measures and reactions didn't wait. Some merchants, to avoid taxes, engaged in smuggling and opted for a boycott of British products. In the case of the colonists, they took advantage of this situation to organize themselves even more and create organizations, such as the Sons of Liberty, to fight for Independence.

What aggravated the situation was when the Townshend Acts were established in 1767 and 1768. This act included a series of taxes on tea, lead, paper, and other imported items. In turn, this caused a series of acts of resistance like more violent protests, refusals to pay, and growing hostility toward the British authorities.

As a result of the subversive behavior of the colonists, the Parliament of Great Britain decided to enact the famous Intolerable Acts. This only worsened the situation of opposition and further unified the colonies, which were encouraged to come together to create the First Continental Congress in 1774.

The members of Congress attempted to reach an agreement to eliminate the Intolerable Laws, and a letter was sent to King George III to stop taxing the colonists; but the British Crown resisted, which resulted in more confrontations and a series of battles we will describe below.

A Series of Unexpected Events

Arguably the first major battle was of Lexington and Concord in 1775 in Massachusetts. This American victory forced the British to begin a retreat to Boston.

It was followed by a series of warlike confrontations where the Patriots were testing their strategies to be able to defeat the British Army, which after all was one of the most powerful armed forces in the world. To this would be added the Declaration of Independence. It was approved in July 1776 and contained the complaints of colonial citizens against the British government.

What would undoubtedly make the difference in the development of the war for the independence of the United States would be the battle of Saratoga in 1777.

The U.S. Army, which was made up of lower and middle-class people, managed to ambush the British, which ended up working. This ambush forced the general in command of the British to surrender in October 1777, which caused France to join the war in support of the American cause.

Thus, the situation would become an international conflict with the intervention of France, and later Spain.

The role of the French in the Battle of Yorktown was key to finally putting an end to the major armed conflicts and beginning negotiations with Great Britain.

What definitively ended the conflict was the Treaty of Paris in 1783, where the independence of the United States was formally recognized and the territory was ceded to the new country.

Prominent Figures and the Road to Freedom

As with any event of great relevance like the American Revolution, some characters appear to change the course of things and make a difference. Throughout this struggle, which would last about eight years, there were some names worth mentioning. We cannot overlook the leadership of George Washington. He was the Commander in Chief of the Continental Army. The victory of the Patriots in the American War of independence is due in large part to his great performance.

Another important character is Thomas Jefferson, the principal author of the Declaration of Independence. He defended his ideals of individual liberty and democracy to the hilt and represented Virginia during the War of Independence.

Benjamin Franklin would also help draft and sign the Declaration of Independence. He would lead the campaign to repeal the aforementioned Stamp Act. His work would also be crucial in gaining the support of France in the last years of the American Revolution.

Likewise, we must mention Thomas Peine, who from his position as editor-in-chief of a magazine, wrote the famous pamphlet called *Common Sense.* In this document, he questioned the institutionality of the British Crown and especially the role of George III.

Patrick Henry and his speeches also contributed to expressing the feelings of the colonists. Due to his excellent speech-making skills, he was in charge of requesting Congress for the official Declaration of Independence, as well as serving at many other occasions during the War.

Effects of the War

As mentioned earlier, the Peace of Paris ended the war. The United States of America was recognized as an independent nation.

The American Revolution was the first triumph against a European Empire and was the reference model for future Republican nations that would have a Democratic model of government.

The impact would have on an international level would be great, specifically in the initiation of the Atlantic Revolutions. It was also the beginning of a nation where the struggle for the rights and liberties of certain minorities would gain strength, as was the case of African Americans, women, and Native Americans.

As a consequence, there would also be losses of territories by the majority of Native Americans as the nation expanded westward. There would be a separation between Church and

State. And years later, the abolition of slavery in the Northern States of the United States of America.

Presentation of the Book

The people who lived during this conflict had to make many changes in their way of life in search of that longed-for dream of freedom and autonomy.

Among the challenges they had to face, they put their ideals to the test, had to face the distance from their loved ones, and make decisions in challenging contexts, putting aside their interests and helping their community. Facing these adverse circumstances helped many of them to realize their great capacity to help one another, to bring out a unique inner strength, and to perform acts of courage and kindness.

As a passionate writer about children's literature, I want you to learn about these stories that many do not know about the American Revolution so that they serve as inspiration and motivation for little readers, like you, based on the lessons learned by ten different characters in the course of an event as shocking as war.

Chapter 1

An Unparalleled Heroic Act

Because no matter what they say, you always have a choice.
You just don't always have the guts to make it.
–Ray N. Kuili

The main character of this story was born in Fredericksburg, New York. Sybil Ludington was her name, and she belonged to a middle-class family. She was the oldest of seven siblings so she was used to supporting her mother and helped take care of her younger siblings.

Sybil was the daughter of Colonel Henry Ludington, who had served more than 60 years for the British Army but decided to switch to the Patriot's side during the American Revolution.

She lived a relatively quiet life on a farm between Connecticut and the Long Island shore. There she had learned to ride horses as part of her duties, and due to her father's active role in her community, she also helped him from time to time with some chores related to his work in the militia. From a very young age, she showed interest in community affairs and it can be said that she was a very energetic and active girl.

Both she and her mother supported the Patriot's cause as best they could, acting as sentries during the night to watch for movements near the farm where they lived. They also provided shelter from time to time for Patriot sympathizers. Sometimes they even joined the neighbors to make clothes since they refused to consume English products.

However, that active role in supporting the cause would grow, making Sybil take a leading role in the freedom fight one night in April 1777.

Trouble is Brewing

It was an April afternoon in 1777 at the Ludington home when a loud knock was heard at the door. Sybil suddenly felt her heart race, as if she had a hunch and a strong feeling about her future and that of her family.

It was a messenger who, with much regret, would inform Sybil and her relatives that British troops were attacking and invading the nearby town of Danbury. This city was an important source of supplies for the Continental Army (as the 13 American colonies were called) and its location allowed a passage between cities; thus, its invasion meant a great casualty for the Patriots.

Unfortunately, on that rainy April afternoon, the British soldiers had caused great losses for the American colonists, especially in economic matters.

You could imagine how upset the Ludingtons were to hear this sad news. There was nothing they could do, but they had to act quickly to warn their people of possible attacks and join the Continental Army to follow the corresponding plan of action.

The Night of the Ride

Feeling the weight of the world on your shoulders at 16 is not something that happens very often. That is what Sybil would feel later that night as she ventured out on a risky night ride where many things would be at stake.

The messenger was the leader of a local militia of farmers and laborers. He was requesting the help of Colonel Ludington and his men, who numbered an average of 400, to engage the British forces. Unfortunately for him, the colonel's men were scattered around the area in their respective haciendas and hamlets, so someone would have to go and round them up in the middle of the night.

But who could it be if the first one was exhausted after having made a long journey to get there and bring them the message? His strength would not allow him to resist another long journey, and Sybil's father needed to stay so he could greet each man who arrived. It was his responsibility to make a plan and get everyone organized as soon as possible; after all, he was their leader.

The minutes passed, and the alternatives were not many. Sybil, witnessing such an alarming situation and being aware of what it could mean not to summon her father's militia in time, gathered up her courage. Without thinking of anything else, she volunteered.

You can imagine her father's face and the surprise this represented for the messenger who was with them, as well as for her mother and younger siblings. They were all dumbfounded and speechless. They had no doubts whatsoever about the young woman's skills as a rider and her knowledge of the surrounding roads, but that did not take away from how risky the journey through those dark, leafy woods could be.

The first thing that came to her father's mind was to take his daughter away from the rest and have a private conversation.

"My daughter, are you sure you want to do this? I don't want you to feel forced to do something you don't feel sure about," her father asked, full of fear and pride inside.

To which she replied, "It is something I must do, for us, for our people, and besides, it is the only chance we have to get rid of a possible British attack. I am convinced it is worth it."

Thus, a few minutes passed in silence until her father accepted his daughter's offer by stressing the following to her, "Honey, you know we will be here for whatever you need. If you see that things get tough, do not hesitate to come back. Whatever happens, we will face it together."

"Don't worry, Dad. I will keep it in mind, and I appreciate your concern. Love you very much," replied the 16-year-old girl.

"I love you very much too," her dad whispered, his voice cracking.

With an accumulation of mixed feelings, the teenager's parents and others present watched the young Sybil leave for a unique and risky adventure. Pride, sorrow, anguish, and hope was what her parents felt as they said goodbye to her before she began her journey.

An Odyssey of a Journey

Through the lush forest, with a light rain accompanying her, Young Sybil was determined to fulfill her mission. Riding at full speed and without hesitation, that teenager carried a great responsibility with her. The young girl was traveling alone, without any company or any kind of major protection, such as an escort.

On top of that, the horse she was riding, named Estrella, had a saddle a little bigger than she was used to for a girl of her size and parts of the roads were wet due to the rain. In other words, she had several factors working against her that made that ride the longest and riskiest of all.

Her mind wanted to play a trick on her, bringing with it the image of that group of British soldiers who wandered through the vast fields. It was inevitable to wonder: what would happen if they found her?

Surely there were moments of doubt and uncertainty, moments in which she would ask herself: *What time will I get home? Will I meet someone on the way? What do I do if I see a British soldier?*

But she would quickly come back to reality, and only one thing remained in her mind–the fight for freedom. If they could stop the British from invading the surrounding areas, it would be a small victory for the biggest victory of all: Freedom from British rule.

Her bravery was due to his great hope to see her country become a new nation and to get new opportunities for the settlers. Although not everything would happen so quickly, this was a big step toward it. One more step to be climbed to advance toward the longed-for independence.

That kept the Fredericksburg teenager awake most of the night, knocking on the doors of the houses scattered throughout the countryside, keeping them on alert, and summoning the Colonel's men to battle. At the sight of her, the families of those men could not help but wonder who the young lady was and stand admiring her great galloping prowess. It was a sight to behold and would remain in the memory of the surrounding neighbors for a lifetime.

On average, Sybil rode about 40 miles in total that night, almost three times as much as Paul Revere's famous ride. Thus demonstrating her great riding prowess, but even more so her enormous commitment to the Patriot cause and her great concern to protect her people from a possible British threat.

Neither the weather nor the bad conditions of the journey deterred the 16-year-old girl, who already knew the layout of the land in the surrounding area as she had accompanied her father to some of his meetings with his men and knew where they were located. Without thinking she had been preparing for that moment for some time.

Mission Accomplished

It was not long before dawn when Sybil was finally able to return home safely and, as expected, felt very exhausted but with a happy and satisfied heart.

Meanwhile, the men her father worked with were already gathering in the vicinity and the militia was preparing to join other Continental Army units on their way to Connecticut.

Sybil's great effort was applauded and appreciated by her neighbors, friends, and locals. Her family was quick to show their admiration and respect for her. In fact, in gratitude, some neighbors and friends got together to organize a celebration for her. The tributes would continue years later as the story became better known. Sybil's humble character embraced the tributes with prudence and sympathy.

From that day forward, her father reaffirmed that he considered her a great ally for the fight and that he had decided that she was ready to accompany him on several of his missions, in addition to giving her his support to continue training as a rider.

The significance of Sybil's feat inspired many others to fight for the freedom of their country, and showed that not only great leaders can be heroes and demonstrate great courage in protecting their own. It showed that age or gender doesn't matter when it comes to performing an act of bravery and great vigor.

It would take several years for the British forces to surrender in October 1781 and end the war. The story of this brave young woman would not be known until almost 60 years later, but it certainly shows us that great deeds are not only performed by well-known people or people with great positions.

Lessons Learned

- Among the values that stand out the most in young Sybil are her courage and contribution to her community. Her sense of belonging to her people and the desire to help the Patriotic cause made the young woman take the risk that night in April.

- Fortunately in Sybil's case, despite the adversities of the road, she was able to complete her journey; but if it had not been so, it would still be worthy of admiration since she gave her all to achieve her goal. There would have been nothing wrong if she had returned halfway because she considered it to be too dangerous. After all, everyone knows their abilities and weaknesses and must make the decision that best suits them.

- Sybil's strength while riding showed how much she cared about protecting the ones she loved the most. She was aware of the great danger of riding, but her love for her family made her want to contribute to the mission. It is not necessary to risk our lives to show our love and affection to those we love, but this act was certainly worth more than a thousand words.

- External conditions will not always be in our favor to achieve our most desired dreams or goals, but we can draw strength to counteract them and focus on what we want. These factors should not discourage us, but rather motivate us to ask ourselves: What am I willing to do to fight for my goals? What would I be willing to give up for it?

- Family unity is also worthy of note in this family, as each one contributed in the home or outside it in any way they could. In this case, it was Sybil, but if it had been the mission, no doubt another member could have also taken a more active role.

Chapter 2

Union Make Force

As you grow older, you will discover that you have two hands - one for helping yourself, the other for helping others.
–Audrey Hepburn

Despite being a man of African-American descent, future businessman and abolitionist James Forten was born and raised a free man in Philadelphia in 1766. His grandfather had been a man freed from slavery years earlier, meaning he was able to enjoy this privilege.

As a young boy, he had to work to take care of his mother and sister after his father died in a boating accident when he was 9-years-old. So he took on great responsibility at a young age, leaving behind his Quaker background (a religious sect characterized by mystical devotion, rejection of violence and war, and strong support for humanitarian and charitable causes, etc.) to attend a school where he was educated under the direction of abolitionist Anthony Benezet.

This, however, did not prevent him from continuing his studies on his own. He took advantage of the little free time he had to catch up on the subjects that corresponded to him according to his school year.

Problems on Board

When he was only 14-years-old, he went to sea and served on a ship named Royal Louis, which was commanded by Stephen Decatur, a sailor who supported the United States during the Revolutionary War.

On the first voyage, everything went wonderfully: they had managed to capture several British ships. But unfortunately, they did not have the same luck on a second voyage in 1781. This time, while Forten was transporting gunpowder from the ship's powder magazine to the cannons, the ship he was on was captured by two British ships called *HMS Nymphe* and *HMS Amphion*.

After this event, the risk of Forten being sold as a slave was very high. Fortunately, instead, he was transferred to the *HMS Jersey*, where he became a prisoner of war. However, he managed to impress the captain of the ship, who made sure that his crew treated James like any other white prisoner of war.

Living conditions on the ship were very harsh. Access to good food and hygiene was virtually impossible. So young Forten did what he could to cope with the situation. Fortunately, he befriended John Beazley, the ship's captain, who offered Forten a way off the ship and the opportunity to move to England and join the British side.

What would you have done? Well, in the case of this young man, doubts did not get the better of him and he decided to refuse the offer. His decline demonstrated how important it was for him to remain on the side of the revolutionary cause and stand with the rest of his fellow Patriots–even if it meant living under precarious conditions. For him, it was more important to be loyal to his struggle for freedom and provide support to his shipmates.

"Comrade Forten, you don't know how much we appreciate what you have done for us. Being so far away from your family, I imagine that this decision must not have been easy to make. And we really want you to know that, despite being in these conditions, it is people like you who make us feel every day that the longed-for freedom will come soon. That everything will have been worth it and that we have each other at this time. You can always count on our support," one of his companions told him. This undoubtedly made him aware of the appreciation and respect they had for him every day.

"Dear fellow Patriots, I value your words very much and wish that this uncertainty ends soon so that we can return to our lands and make a better future for our community. I will always do what is in my hands to defend my own from injustices, do not doubt it; and I could not question my ideals and my convictions because I, more than anyone, want to see this nation free and with the freedom that corresponds to it."

As we can see, the loyalty and commitment James showed to the cause were worthy of admiration; from a very young age, he was already clear about what he wanted and was willing to fight for it. It is worth remembering that during the time of the Revolution, the stakes were high for African Americans. The British would do anything to be able to unite more men in their army. So much so that they offered freedom to the men enslaved during the war.

Facing that dilemma must have been hard for many, and we do not judge those who accepted it as it was a very difficult situation. But this was not the case for James, it was clear to him who he should support, and he proved it by his decision to stay on the ship as a prisoner. James remained a prisoner for seven more months and was then released.

New Beginnings

Sometime after his release, he began working in the sail-making industry in Philadelphia, mentored by a man named Robert who was an expert in the field. He would teach him everything he knew about it, and so it would not be long before James became successful in the industry.

James was a very disciplined young man and very skilled in everything he did. He put a lot of effort into his work, ergo, it is not surprising that he ended up being the foreman of the store where he worked at the age of 20. He had established a friendly relationship with the owner, who trusted him completely for any assignment he needed. One way or another, Mr. Robert was grooming James to take over the business in the future.

And so it was, after Mr. Robert's retirement, James became the new manager of the business. He assumed this position with great responsibility and commitment as Robert would have expected. The service provided by young Forten in the store was of excellent quality and also added innovative techniques for handling candles.

All of this made the business grow, and as a result, made James a wealthy man. In addition, it should be noted that as a boss, he was very fair with his workers. He always made sure that they felt comfortable in their work and that they received equal treatment, regardless of their race. In his business, he employed black and white workers without distinction.

An Active Struggle for Equality

One of the reasons why James joined the revolutionaries was to fight for the freedom not only of the American colonists, but also to promote the cause of his people of race. He saw independence as the most viable way to dream of the longed-for freedom of African Americans nationwide.

He used his privileged position at the time to fight against slavery and demand the rights of African Americans. As a businessman, he began to connect with more people and took advantage of the connections he made to raise his voice and reach more people.

After he established himself, Forten became increasingly involved in political activism in favor of black civil rights. Mostly, after the strong discrimination they suffered in Pennsylvania and Northern states because they didn't have the right to vote and to be part of juries.

In this way, he also became involved in journalism and decided to invest in the newspaper *The Liberator*, where he wrote and published a series of letters under the title *Letters from a Colored Man*, which was published anonymously. James denounced a bill that required all black emigrants to Pennsylvania to be registered in the state and participated in several protests for equal treatment in favor of the African-American community.

Here is an excerpt from one of his letters on a Late Bill Before The Senate Of Pennsylvania:

"We hold this truth to be self-evident that God created all men equal, and is one of the most prominent features in the Declaration of Independence and in that glorious fabrication of collected wisdom, our noble Constitution.

This idea embraces the Indian and European, the Savage and the Saint, the Peruvian and the Laplander, the White Man and the African, and whatever measures are adopted subversive of this inestimable privilege, are in direct violation of the letter and spirit of our Constitution, and become subject to the animadversion of all, particularly those who are deeply interested in the measure (Forten, 1766-1842)."

In one of James' letters, he mentions that the bill violated the rights of any free black and that it discriminated against them for not being equal to whites. What he meant by this was that the citizens of the black community should be recognized and valued.

He remained active for many more years, teaming up with the bishop of a Methodist Church to organize a mass meeting to discuss issues relevant to the community. Whenever he could, he would meet with the members of his community so he would be aware of their problems and celebrate any small advances they had made.

Community, First and Foremost

James arguably took on a community leadership role by being one of the most listened to and respected voices in Philadelphia. He was strongly opposed to the emigration of African American. He asserted with conviction that blacks should have an equal role as any other citizen in his homeland of the United States.

The years did not pass in vain, and he became very skilled in dealing with the press. Being involved in the media himself, it was easier for him to get contacts, to know the availability of certain journalists, etc. He was very strategic when it came to choosing his schedule. He knew when to step back and when to push for something.

It was as if all the events of his life had prepared him more and more for what he was experiencing at that point in his adulthood. He had witnessed firsthand the mistreatment of his community, and he was far from indifferent. On the contrary, it motivated him to stay active and involved which made his community also appreciate him and consider him as a representative worthy of their respect and sympathy.

James remained active as long as he could, and without a doubt, his activism, great empathy, and fighting spirit served as an inspiration for the next generations of blacks in Philadelphia. Years later, honors and tributes were to follow but beyond that, the gratitude and the changes that happened thanks to James' character remained in the memory of the black community for life.

Lessons Learned

- It is admirable of the great kindness that James had since he was a child, always prevailing the needs of others for his own. As a child, he had to take care of his mother and sister, and later during his stay as a prisoner on a ship of the British, decided to stay with the rest of his companions despite the offer he would receive to go to England. He put his commitment to the revolutionary cause and support for the rest of the prisoners on the ship ahead of his safety and personal benefits.

- His commitment was also noticeable in his work, gaining the trust of his boss in a short time and then taking charge of it. It shows us that if we do things the right way and put our all into them, we can achieve great results.

- He understood that for his fight for the rights of the black community to gain more strength, it was necessary to have allies and work together. In order to do so, he gathered people interested in his efforts and organized several activities that made visible what it meant to be an African American in the northern cities of the United States.

- When you have a vocation of service and a great passion for what you do as James did, it is natural to think that you will want to remain active for a long time.

Chapter 3

Family Life in Wartime

In family life, love is the oil that eases friction, the cement that binds closer together, and the music that brings harmony. –
Friedrich Nietzsche

L ittle was previously known about the lives of the wives of high-ranking wartime commanders, as they either went unnoticed or generated little interest. However, this chapter will be devoted to one of the most loyal and committed family lives of those known, Lucy Flucker.

Lucy Knox was a woman who came from the Flucker family: a Massachusetts high-society family. Her father held a position in the British colonial government, so she had several privileges.

She was fortunate to have a quality education, something that was not very common at the time. In addition, she had access to a good amount of resources in the library at home. So since she was a child, her curiosity for books was awakened. It was on one of her walks through the city of Boston, where she lived, that she met her future husband. He owned a small bookstore in front of Cornhill, a place frequented by British officers. The two connected very well, and began to frequent each other soon after.

Lucy attracted a lot of attention because she was a very cultured woman, with many topics of conversation, quick, and clever. At the same time, she was very kind to those around her and knew how to have fun. All this did not go unnoticed by the young Henry, who, after a few years, proposed to her.

In 1774, she married Henry Knox, which brought her problems with her family since her parents wanted her to marry someone of a higher social status and similar political views. That was the first big challenge they would have to go through to stay together, but several more were soon to follow.

Changes in Sight

Lucy and her husband left Boston after the British occupied it. Despite an offer made by the British to Henry to join their cause, he flatly refused.

From that moment on, Lucy supported her husband as much as she could when he became an active member in the struggle for independence. On the way to the Continental Army camp, Lucy had sewn a sword into her cloak to protect them from any incidents.

She was always on the lookout for any threat, because she knew that as Patriots they would be perfect targets for the British. Her life would undergo a series of changes from then on. Among them, the main thing would be to face the distance in the rawest moments of the war.

Constantly on the move to the battlefields, they chose to live in rented housing as their family grew.

Despite being married, they spent much of the Revolutionary War apart. The main reason was that her husband, in an effort to protect her, refused to allow her to go to the war camps so often. Not wanting her to be a witness to what was going on there, which was very hard, he knew she was at risk of being exposed to a British soldier if they were to see her.

This situation was difficult for Lucy to accept, since she was always on the lookout for events and Henry's welfare. Several times she had to deal with the uncertainty of not knowing where he was or what his next move would be. But she was confident that she would soon find out, as he always told her everything that was happening in great detail in his letters.

Family Union

Perhaps one of the most difficult events Lucy had to go through was the birth of her first daughter, since Henry could not be present. Of course, he was aware of her; but it wasn't the same. Fortunately, Lucy had made a couple of good friends, who were also other wives of Henry's comrades on the front lines. They perfectly understood what young Lucy was going through, and they were the ones who recommended that she go to her family so that she would feel more support.

After several years of being somewhat incommunicado with her siblings and parents, Lucy decided it was time to reach out and introduce them to the newborn baby girl. It was a rather touching moment that also demonstrated what a great human being Lucy had become, able to put aside past quarrels and join forces for what was best for her little girl.

From time to time, she left them to her family but as her life was very nomadic, it was not as often as she would have preferred.

In any case, that reconciliation with her family only gave Lucy more strength to go ahead with her plan to keep her family together as best she could.

In one of those conversations she had with his sister, she confessed her feelings for what she was going through:

"Oh my sister, with all my heart, I hope this war will end soon. This distance is hard, not only in my case but also in the case of other families who are going through the same thing. When will this end? Only God knows. What I do know for sure is that I will take advantage of the little time I have when we are all together to have more fun, enjoy the company of good friends, and celebrate the worthwhile moments," Lucy said.

"Of course, I understand you, my dear Lucy. However, we will manage to go see you wherever you are as soon as we can. Meanwhile, we will be watching over you and the little one. You know that whatever you may need, you can count on our support. A big hug from afar, take care of yourself," her sister said.

Unbreakable Bonds

During wartime, Henry and Lucy maintained good communication with each other through regular letters. Between them, they would write things like the following:

"Adored Lucy, I miss you and those beautiful children we have so much. I would give anything to be with you at this moment, but duty prevents me. I hope you are feeling as well as the last time we spoke, and with that unique strength that characterizes you, you will see how soon we will get together to celebrate those small victories we are having with the rest of the American soldiers and their families.

I thank you infinitely for all the support you always give me. You are a key piece in this, my accomplice in every step I take. A hug to infinity, your adored Henry."

Here is another fragment from another letter:

"I feared a lot for your safety in the last battle. You don't know what difficult news I was receiving, the anguish I felt was great, but I am relieved to receive your letters and that you tell me of your next steps. Remember I will always be here for you. With love, Lucy."

As we can see the connection between the two of them was very strong. They had a lot of confidence between them to express what they were feeling, and some of their sorrows. Although they went through hard things, they always did it together, giving each other support when they needed it.

A Festive Spirit

Lucy spent much of the war in friends' homes or rented houses. But whenever she could she would go to camp, no matter how harsh the conditions, she wanted to see her family together.

So every visit was essential for her, and she made the most of it. There she was the one who organized the meetings among the soldiers, making her stay, and that of the other families, very pleasant.

Lucy was very sociable and friendly. It made sense that she was in charge of every entertainment that took place there. You could say that she was the spirit of the camps, which made her husband feel very fortunate to have her by his side. Her way of contributing to the cause of not losing joy in the middle of a war was just what was needed in those times.

Of course, she was very respectful of the laws of the Army. She knew the times that were available to celebrate and was very cautious in the type of meetings she organized, always taking into account the welfare of the families and the comfort of all those present in the camp.

Something that should also be emphasized is that she was very independent. Not only because of the time she spent alone taking care of her children with occasional help from her friends or siblings from time to time, but also in making her own decisions. Especially when it came to coordinating her visits, sometimes it was difficult to agree, but she knew well when it was worth the risk and when it wasn't.

From everything Henry told her, she was getting to know more about military strategy and could predict some movements of the opposing side.

In addition, she would also make connections with other important military wives who contributed to the Patriot cause. Among them, the one that stood out the most was her friendship with Martha Washington. They remained united in the face of the big criticism received by her husband General George Washington, demonstrating her loyalty not only to her nuclear family but also to her dearest friends.

A Love That Stood the Test of Time

For Henry, the safety of his family was paramount, so he did not want them to take a greater risk with other visitors. Both were important emotional support in each other's lives. They were together at key moments, such as the reading of the Declaration of Independence, and the hardest moments, like the taking of New York City.

Although Lucy had been raised in a very well-off family and had not lacked anything material, she did not mind living a distant life to support her husband.

It was demonstrated that her love for her family was bulletproof and that she adapted as best she could to a new life in that historical moment of the American nation.

Neither the distance nor the events of war challenged Henry and Lucy's feelings about staying together and wanting to spend time with their loved ones.

After the war, Lucy's life became more stable. She returned to Boston, where she had grown up and bought a large piece of land with Henry. It was on that land that they built a suitable home and spent some time together. After a few years, they finally settled in the south of France, where they finally had the quiet life they had longed for years before.

Lessons Learned

- Lucy proved her loyalty to Henry at the beginning of the story by marrying him despite her family's opposition, following in his footsteps with the Continental Army, and always looking out for his and her children's welfare.

- There may be times when we may have to be physically separated from our loved ones, but that does not mean that we are cut off from them or that we do not continue to care for them. Whenever we can, especially in this technological age, we can make time to catch up and talk to them through whatever means of communication we find most appropriate. As happened to Lucy and Henry, who kept in touch and were honest with each other through letters, they did not miss what was going on in each other's lives.

- The reconciliation of Lucy and her family after the birth of her firstborn shows that it is good to give second chances in life and to leave aside feelings, such as resentment. Whenever possible it is better to settle past issues with those whom we had some mishap or estrangement with and try to repair the relationship or emotional bond.

- It is remarkable the cheerful spirit that characterized Lucy, especially in those hard times. That made her very well-liked in Henry's circle, and she was able to relieve the tensions felt by the soldiers and their families.

Chapter 4

Dicey's Courage

Courage is very important.
Like a muscle, it is strengthened by use.
–Ruth Gordon

Laodicea Langston, better known as Dicey to her inner circle, was a Revolutionary War Patriot who was born and raised on her father's plantation in South Carolina.

Small in stature, dark-eyed, and with a glowing attitude, the 15-year-old Dicey was an excellent markswoman and horsewoman with great riding skills.

Left in the care of her father and siblings after the early death of her mother, the young girl grew up to be a warrior. She was willing to help her brothers in any way she could when they decided to leave the house to fight with the Continental Army.

Although they couldn't see each other very often, the siblings managed to keep in touch with their family through Dicey. She would slip away from time to time to give them reach wherever they were, be it in the middle of the forest or over a long distance.

Danger in Sight

As young Dicey went about her daily chores, she would sometimes notice British troops lurking near her father's farm, so she would always record everything they did. She would then relay information to the camp where her brothers were.

It is worth noting that his father was a fervent Patriot, and whenever he could, he helped his neighbors and donated some of the natural products he grew on his plantations. Several of them were loyal to the British Crown, so Dicey would obtain more information about the movements of the opposing side.

That brought a clear advantage to the group in the camp where his brothers were since they could access key information about the future actions of the British. It did not take long to generate suspicion among the bandits, who belonged to the British Conservative Party and decided to threaten Dicey's father so that no more information would be leaked to the Patriots.

Upon learning of this situation, Dicey's father told her, "My daughter, we are facing a group of very dangerous bandits. I know that you care a lot about helping your brothers and other Patriots, but I ask you to please stop passing on information. For your protection and that of our land, we will see how we can help them and keep up to date with what is happening."

The young Dicey had to agree to her father's request, but this would change when she learned that some bands of British outlaws wanted to attack the camp where her brother, James, and other rebels were. As soon as she found out, the young woman did not hesitate to tell him what they were planning without thinking about her father's orders.

She was worried because she knew how dangerous they could be, and she thought of her brother's welfare before anything else.

To be able to inform him she had to think about how she would escape without anyone noticing her absence. Then it occurred to her to go out at night while everyone was asleep, and go through the forest and fields so she wouldn't be discovered at the camp where her brother James was.

To do that, she also had to cross a river whose icy waters had risen on rainy days. She was very afraid and insecure to go through such a place, but the desire to warn her brother and protect him from possible danger filled her with courage.

She continued along the path, and suddenly, she fell down the river. The waters swept her away and spun her around. She wasn't sure where she was going, but gathered all her strength and slowly made her way to the shore. She stayed there for a while, soaking wet and without much strength; and after a few minutes, she was finally on her way to warn her brother.

She kept going and found the right path. She had to travel a moderately long distance to reach her brother's camp, warning him that they were in danger of being found by the new outlaw scouts. He and his companions had just returned from an expedition they had made and were exhausted.

Although young Dicey had also lost most of her energy on her journey, she helped them light the fire and mixed cornbread to place on the coals. She then broke it into pieces and put them in the men's backpacks so they could eat while they ran to warn the group of settlers who lived nearby.

They were all very grateful for young Dicey's behavior and let her know, stating:

> "We know that it has cost you a lot to get here, and I want you to know that you value your effort very much. Without a doubt, you are a young lady who cares a lot about her family and seeks to defend her own. Thank you very much. Whenever you need it, you can count on us."

"What a great gesture on you Dicey! We needed your help. Don't worry, we will get the message out to as many of the settlers as we can. You have given us the impetus to do so."

After a long and exhausting night, she arrived home in time to prepare breakfast for her unsuspecting father. She had been out all night, and yet she acted as if nothing was wrong and chatted with her dad about various everyday topics. It was several weeks before anyone found out about the risky 20 mile adventure she had taken.

A Very Significant Rescue

As expected, by the time the group of outlaws arrived at the site of the rebel camps, it was too late. Thanks to Dicey's early warning, they had moved to another location, and the place was empty. This only increased the anger and annoyance of the British supporters who began to look at the Langston family as their main suspect.

It wasn't long before the group of outlaws decided it was time for revenge. So one night, they approached his house to attack him and loot his belongings. Salomon, Dicey's father, confronted them and flatly denied any link with the information filter, but they did not believe him and wanted to shoot him.

Dicey witnessed this terrible scene and put herself between her father and the angry outlaw, who warned her to back off or face the consequences. She began to exclaim fervently that her father was a sick old man. She clung to her father, hugging him tightly and ready to defend him from anyone who tried to harm him.

The scene was very touching to the point that one of the bandits was convinced that the young woman was right, and that they should spare the old man. It seems that Dicey's efforts served to make them come to their senses and stopped them from retaliating against her father.

When the bandits finally retreated, Dicey and her father embraced for a long time, and he could not hold back the tears of emotion in gratitude for his daughter's quick thinking. Dicey was in shock and could not believe what had just happened. It took a few hours for her to finally come to her senses and admire the courage she had shown in order to save her father from those men.

She could only tell him how much she loved him and how relieved she was that they were both safe. That day they also thanked Dicey's mother in Heaven for protecting them. Even though she had passed away when she was a little girl, she was still present in the most meaningful moments of their lives, just Dicey and her father.

Dicey's Exploits

On another occasion, the young Dicey was riding her horse back home from a neighboring settlement in the Spartanburg district when she was suddenly stopped by a group of loyalists (settlers who were in favor of the British Crown).

"Miss Dicey, we have heard of you. We know that your brothers have joined the Patriot side, and you have contact with them. We demand that you tell us about it! Otherwise, you will face the consequences," one of them said, raising his voice.

She replied, "I know nothing about it, I assure you!"

But the loyalist didn't believe her and threatened to harm her if she didn't tell him. But far from scaring her with these insinuations, Dicey managed to say, "I don't care if you don't believe me, I won't tell you!"

Again he insisted that she tell him, and once again she refused. He was enraged and wanted to attack her when another member of the group jumped to her defense, causing the men to argue. Taking advantage of distraction, Dicey, who was still on her horse, decided to make her escape.

It had been a while since Dicey had saved her father from a group of outlaws. Instead of frightening her and making her stop supporting the Patriot side, it strengthened her and she became more battle-hardened. But there would be several more occasions where she would face bands of loyalists who sought to intimidate her and her family.

Dicey's attitude did not go unnoticed by the surrounding neighbors and other loyalists, who knew that she was a teenager with a lot of courage, brave enough to defend the possessions of her family, and help anyone who served the cause.

Post-War Life

When life was calmer in the interior of the country, Dicey married a young man named Thomas when she was only 16-years-old. They moved to a county in the city of Greenville, where they would have a traditional family life and many children.

They dedicated themselves mainly to agricultural activity; Dicey already had experience with it since she always helped at home with the chores on the land. The husband was a founder of the nearby Jackson Grove United Methodist Church, so it was a place frequented by the family.

The now-wife, Dicey kept her memories of all those adventures she had lived through during the war of independence. She always instilled the importance of fighting for what they believed in to her children; and that from time to time, it was worth taking risks if it was to protect their loved ones or to defend their ideals.

She told them some of her stories and experiences, both the good and the bad, so that they would learn to defend themselves in life and not be afraid to face challenges when it was their turn to do so. She also taught her girls that no one should minimize them because they were women and that they, like their brothers, were capable of defending their families and had the skills of warriors–just as Dicey did in her younger years.

Lessons Learned

- It is important to highlight Dicey's audacity to face the most dangerous situations and come out successful. However, we must take into account that, although the reasons why she took those actions are valid, we must also take into account the circumstances she lived in and the skills she already had because of the way she was raised. Not all of us are capable of it.

- Her fighting spirit was also due in large part to the love she had for her family, and wanting to protect them no matter what. If it was within her means she would do anything to support them, whether it was giving them information, taking care of the farm, or taking on groups of loyalists and outlaws who wanted to rob them or attack them.

- The relationship she had with her father was very special, as he always took care of her and taught her to defend herself from a young age. He was the closest person she had, so she defended him as best she could and took care of him when she was older while her brothers were in hiding when they joined the Patriot cause. She showed him with her actions how much he meant to her and her gratitude for having taken care of her after her mother's death.

Chapter 5

A Well-Kept Secret

You never know how strong you are,
until being strong is your only choice.
–Bob Marley

Early Years

There are stories worth telling, and Deborah Sampson's is certainly one of them. She was born into a humble family of seven children, descending from pre-eminent Pilgrims. Unfortunately, due to financial problems and after the disappearance of Jonathan, the father of the Sampson family, Deborah's mother had to place her children in different homes.

In Deborah's case, she worked from the age of ten for the family of Benjamin Thomas. He was a farmer from Middleborough, Massachusetts with a large family. So she was accompanied by the farmer's children, with whom she played with and talked to in her free time.

While there, she studied on her own for her school year. One of the sons tutored her in some of the subjects in which she had doubts. They would get together to study and support each other.

That is how she improved her studies; and at the age of 18, when she could become independent, she decided to work as a teacher in a nearby school where she had been offered a temporary job for the summer vacation in 1779.

She also got another job as a weaver, a skill her mother had taught her from an early age. She quickly became a very skilled weaver and was sought after by several of the wealthiest families in the town of Middleborough. She managed as best she could, was very independent, and fend for herself.

Occasionally, she would also send her loving siblings, with whom she had grown up with on the farm, a little something. She was very kind and liked to share as much as she could.

An Unexpected Turn

During those years, a series of clashes would begin between American rebels seeking independence from the United States and British soldiers. Thus, she started to get involved in political activism and gradually became a Patriot.

In 1782, Sampson enlisted for the Continental Army under the assumed name Robert Shurtleff. "He" joined the Massachusetts Infantry Company under the command of George Webb. Before deciding to join the group, , she had one of her brothers from the farm help her change her appearance. Hehelped her hide her feminine features under her clothes, taught her to modulate her voice differently, and recommended what type of hairstyle to wear.

Already in combat, she belonged to one of the most active troops in the Hudson Valley. Deborah, as a member of the Light Infantry Troops, had to be able to maintain a fast and steady marching pace. Plus, she didn't travel with many supplies and was mostly involved in short, somewhat experienced, missions.

She had leadership qualities and was very dedicated to her work. Fortunately for her, her companions did not suspect her true identity as she knew how to keep it hidden. Occasionally, she would get injured during a mission, and a colleague offered to help her. Sampson would say that she could do it on her own and that they should not worry about treating her.

What Deborah did was to learn on her own to bandage her wounds; and only when she needed a lot of help, she would let them assist her. But she was always very careful not to let them know her identity. Sampson, as her companions told her , needed to keep a strong and bold appearance.

Neutral Ground stretched across what would become today's Westchester County. It was there that Sampson spent most of her time when she was with the Continental Army. It was a zone free of armed combat, where from time to time, some of the most important commanders of the Revolutionary War went to rest or plan their next moves.

George Washington, one of the most well-known figures of the Revolutionary War, spent much of his time north of this area. Sampson was nearby as she had taken a temporary job as a waitress for a well-known general. She did this in her spare time when she wasn't busy on a mission.

Identity Uncovered

While at Neutral Ground, Sampson maintained her job as a waitress and kept busy engaging in occasional confrontations with some loyalist looters. In one of these encounters, someone shot her in the shoulder.

She went into a state of alarm and didn't know what to do. For if she sought proper medical care, they would surely find out the truth. She continued walking, heading to her next mission when she passed out on the way.

It was 1783 when one of her companions found her lying on the ground and quickly took her to a hospital. The attending physician, Barnabas Binney, discovered her and revealed her identity to General Paterson in a letter. The truth of who she was became known, and she was honorably discharged from West Point in October of that same year. Sampson's comrades were very surprised and could not believe that she kept this secret for such a long time.

They were extremely proud and approached her to congratulate her, this time addressing her by her real name:

"Miss Sampson, we are very impressed with this news; and on behalf of the Infantry group, we want to express our congratulations to you for all the commitment and effort you put into every mission. You were one of us and were there whenever we needed. What you did took a lot of courage, and it must have been hard to face it on your own. We were very concerned about your health and also feel comforted that you are recovering."

To which she replied:

"Dear colleagues, I am truly grateful to have belonged to a great group like yours. You always cared about my well-being, regardless of not knowing who I was, and motivated me to be better each time. I appreciate you all very much."

Back Home

After a few months, the war ended and she returned to the town where she grew up in Massachusetts. There she would meet a farmer named Benjamin, whom she married in 1784. Of course, she told him of her great adventure as part of the Infantry troops, and he was amazed at what she had experienced and her great strength.

"I admire your strength of will and the fact that you risked yourself for your homeland. I am very sorry for the moments you had to face alone, but I know you did it for a good reason. I love you very much, and I am proud of you," he always told her.

She felt very good about his words, and his reaction made her realize the great worth of what she had done. That helped her decide to petition the Massachusetts State Legislature for retroactive pay for the time she served in the military.

That act was an important recognition of a woman's work in the military. And it prompted Deborah to embark on a speaking tour of Massachusetts, Rhode Island, and New York. She became a pioneer in this type of activity, where she shared her war experiences and raised her voice for the importance of women in the military and attended dressed in the uniform she wore during her time in the army.

In these lectures, she highlighted the capabilities of women in other non-traditional roles and gave a live demonstration of physically strenuous exercises. Her demonstrations were more convincing than her words, and people could visualize what life was like for a woman in the military.

This series of lectures attracted a lot of attention and made people aware of the equal treatment of women. As a result, Sampson, as her army buddies called her, had become a reference for female empowerment.

She worked there for about a year and then reapplied for a disabled veterans' pension because she had been injured when she was shot in the shoulder and needed support. She had submitted it before but had been unsuccessful. This time the acknowledgment she had gained through touring caused Congress to reverse its decision and grant her application.

The battle Deborah faced in her military service had now shifted to a battle for recognition of the rights of women veterans, who did not have the same benefits as men in that regard. She provided an opportunity to bring this issue into discussion and to make people realize that the country needed to help those who contributed to its founding on equal terms.

As a tribute to Deborah's activism many years later, the Deborah Sampson Act was created, which removed barriers to care and services for many women veterans and ensured that the Department of Veterans Affairs addressed gender gaps.

The act went a long way when it came to addressing the needs of thousands of women veterans who lived in states of neglect and poverty, many of them without adequate medical care. The work Deborah did opened doors to endless opportunities in an effort to improve the lives of female veterans.

In the last years of her life, Deborah spent a lot of time talking about these issues and meeting with other women veterans who had gone through similar situations. They had a lot to say to each other, since the injustices they had experienced were very similar. Fortunately, they had the support of their friends during the war. They helped them demand what was rightfully theirs.

Deborah's legacy lives on in the memory of the people, especially in the state of Massachusetts where Sampson is commemorated with Deborah Sampson Day. There is also a statue of her in front of the city's public library. Some articles have also been published about her experiences in the Army and her fight for equal treatment of women in the field.

Learned Lessons

- Deborah's work reminds us that it is always important to speak up when we consider it necessary to demand our rights. In addition, she remained active in her request for better conditions for the veterans of her community. Also demonstrating her interest in the well-being of her fellow Patriots.

- Deborah did her job as part of the Infantry just as well as any other male soldier. She put a lot of effort into her work and was outstanding in her service. She fought each mission with great courage and fortitude, and was strongly invested in the Patriot cause.

- She was a pioneer in the matter of being one of the first, if not the first, American women to work as a lecturer in some cities of the country, and she was very creative in designing them by doing demonstrations and demanding physical exercises.

- The early life of this war veteran shows us that she learned to be independent at a young age and acquired skills that allowed her to survive. This shows us how resilient humans can be when we find ourselves in challenging circumstances, and that it is good to always be willing to adapt to different situations that come our way. In Deborah's Case, she was adjusting to life on the farm and to a new family, who,luckily for her, treated her well.

- Failure to call for help in time could have cost Deborah her life when she took the bullet in her shoulder. It's understable that she wanted to keep her secret, but when it comes to our health, it is always good to take care of ourselves first.

Chapter 6
A Common Soldier

We, the People, recognize that we have responsibilities as well as rights; that our destinies are bound together; that a freedom which only asks what's in it for me, a freedom without a commitment to others, a freedom without love or charity or duty or Patriotism, is unworthy of our founding ideals, and those who died in their defense.
–Barack Obama

Joseph Plumb Martin is the name of the character in which this story will be based. He was a soldier originally from Massachusetts who was part of the Continental Army for an average of eight years. His war memoirs served to bring us closer to the life of a common soldier in the War of Independence and to assert the rights of war veterans who deserved greater recognition for their work in combat and years of struggle to grant the long-awaited freedom to the United States.

Soldiers like him were key in the victories of the main battles of the Revolutionary War, showing us from the different tasks that he carried out the importance of each function he made and putting the value of working together first.

From Martin, we can also highlight his commitment from an early age to the Patriotic cause and his determination when he enlisted in the Army and faced the opposition of his grandparents, who initially did not want him to join. As we will see throughout this story, this young soldier bravely and courageously demonstrated what he was capable of during his years of service.

The Young Soldier

In those days, it was common for some children to be raised by their grandparents for various reasons. In Joseph's case, it was so that he could receive the best education possible from his grandparents' home in Milford, Connecticut. He had everything he needed. There, the young man developed a great interest in reading and writing, and became very interested in the current events of his country.

Several army recruiters arrived in the town where young Martin was stationed in 1775, shortly after the battles of Lexington and Concord. Some of them stayed at Martin's grandfather's house before they left to join the rest of the soldiers in New York City.

Taking advantage of the proximity, the young Martin, just 15-years-old, had several conversations with the recruits about the benefits of enlisting.

They told him things like, "Young Martin, we have heard great things about you. According to your grandfather, you are a very industrious young man and are in good health. So we feel you would be a good candidate to be part of the Continental Army. Think about it, there is pay involved."

Suddenly Joseph became enthusiastic about the idea and decided to become a soldier. After all, he was being given the opportunity to do something for his country, as well as receive some money in return. At first, his grandparents were not entirely convinced that their grandson should take part in this fight, but they soon realized that there was nothing they could do to change his mind. He was adamant in his decision. Joseph had even told them that if they didn't let him go, he would escape on a warship. Feeling as if they didn't have a choice, they decided to support him in his new adventure by being part of the land service. After all, if he had to do any kind of service, they preferred it to be that.

Thus, without knowing it, Joseph would soon be part of the main battles of the Revolutionary War and would work side-by-side with one of the great leaders of this event of international repercussion: George Washington.

Military Service

His time in the war began in the Connecticut Militia in June 1776, where he was assigned for duty in the New York area. This first period would last until December of that same year. There he gradually adapted to the life of a soldier and earned a good reputation for his great performance.

He returned home before more battles took place and caught up with his family. Afterward, he became part of the

Continental Army in April 1777, serving in the Continental Regiment under General James Varnum. During his time there, he became aware of the sacrifices he would have to make if he wanted to continue serving his country. Despite realizing that living conditions were not entirely liveable, he decided to reaffirm his commitment to the US Army and not turn back.

The commitment he had to his country and the desire to persevere in the fight for independence was so strong that he was willing to tolerate the hardships of war.

Later, he was part of the well-known battles of Brooklyn, White Plains, the siege of Fort Mifflin, and Monmouth. He witnessed violent acts against soldiers of his side and also some victories. He was there for some major losses for the Patriots as well.

He was present during the American Revolution, when the British captured New York City in September 1776. At that time, the city became the British headquarters, and the Continental Army, under the command of General George Washington, had to retreat.

Joseph, who was part of the group, had to move to Washington for the remainder of the war. During that time, he was assigned to the Light Infantry, becoming a corporal because of his leadership and teamwork skills. We can also highlight the fact that he was one of the few literate soldiers in the army, which surely made him stand out and helped him to be assigned more complex tasks.

George Washington had grown fond of the young man for the skills he had demonstrated on the battlefield. He was a very good companion with the rest of the group and was forming a Corps of Sappers and Miners, in which he had to facilitate the movements of his own and his allies' armies to hinder those of the enemy. He was always on the lookout for what he needed to do in order to carry out the plan. Washington gave him the opportunity, and once again proving his great ability in the service, Joseph was promoted to Sergeant. Now, he would be in charge of digging the entrenchments for the Continental Army.

During the War, as we can see, he was part of different types of services, some at the front of the battlefield and others supporting other functions. But what always stood out to his fellow soldiers was Joseph's great aptitude to learn new things and his companionship.

Joseph was also present at the surrender of the British Army at Yorktown, Virginia, a key moment for the end of the Revolutionary War. He remained with Washington for the two years following this event, when the general decided to take his leave of office.

Post-War Years

The cessation of his activities in the Army occurred in June 1773, after remaining in service for almost eight years.

He would then go on to teach in New York for a year. Remember that he was very studious as a young man, and was very cultured since he had had a good education with a big library on hand.

He settled with his wife and children on the Maine frontier, where he became one of the founders of the town of Prospect. Over the years, he was known locally for taking on the role of the farmer, selectman, justice of the peace, and town clerk. Let's just say that everything he had learned in the military served him well in sustaining an impeccable work pace and being very disciplined in whatever work he engaged in.

At this stage of his life, he also dedicated himself to writing stories and an account of his most significant experiences during his military service. Thanks to him, it was possible to obtain more information about the lives of the soldiers of the Revolutionary War. That helped to make visible the work of war veterans, who had not necessarily held high positions and to assert their rights to a decent pension.

War Stories

People said that Joseph carried a journal with him on every mission he undertook, and that it was there that he would write his memoirs. In his journal, he noted that, for a serving soldier, there was no rest between campaigns most of the time. Joseph described it as a continuous routine, Which cost him both emotional and physical wear and tear in his life as a soldier and he would have liked to be able to spend part of the winter with friends and family.

For him, being able to write down what was happening to him in a diary allowed him to unburden himself and express his feelings during the hard battles he lived through. Although when these memoirs were published, they were not taken into account. After more than a century of remaining unnoticed, they were brought to light by George Scheer, a contributor to *American Heritage* magazine.

Unwittingly, what Joseph initially did to please a few friends and acquaintances became a much-talked-about and studied narrative. Joseph's authentic account was one of the first written by privates or junior officers in the early 19th century.

Although Joseph Martin wrote his wartime account in his senior years, the text is fresh, and offers the vision of a young soldier, recounting his struggles and day-to-day efforts and commenting on his successes and disappointments. Remember that while the memoirs are mostly based on a private's perspective, Martin was not one for very long. Rather, he quickly rose through the ranks among the Army's elite troops to corporal, and then sergeant.

So we can conclude that he intended the voice of the common Army worker, who was previously unheard and unheeded, to be heard. That's due in large part to his humility and his desire to help highlight the work of the rank and file.

Undoubtedly, Joseph's stories reveal his cunningness in telling a narrative from the point of view of a not-so-innocent young man who wanted others to know about the injustices that were experienced during wartime. All this was to raise awareness in society to improve living conditions and labor benefits of American soldiers, perhaps thinking of a better future for their fellow Patriots and to please war veterans who, like him, had lived unfortunate experiences in combat.

And just as with these stories, Joseph sought to show the instability of the life of a young soldier, he also demonstrated that he was a Patriot who confessed to having felt immense pride at the final battle of Yorktown, where he witnessed the American flag flying in front of his most implacable adversaries.

As a young soldier, Martin was always very sincere with his opinions, and something that undoubtedly characterized him was his great commitment to his country and his fighting spirit in every combat in which he participated.

Lessons Learned

- From Joseph, we can learn about his desire to get ahead, be very skilled at what he does, and be very committed to the Patriot cause. He left his comforts at home to embark on a new path as part of the Continental Army, knowing what that meant in terms of his lifestyle and customs.

- The commitment and dedication he put into each mission earned him great recognition from his commanders and comrades. He quickly rose through the ranks and witnessed key moments of the American Revolution.

- His war stories allowed us to realize how much he cared about making the voice of the common soldier known, asserting his position, and also contributing to the veteran's community. For it allowed them to be given greater recognition and to assert their rights to retribution for their service.

- We realize with their stories and history how much the soldiers who participated in this conflict sacrificed, from family time, comforts, studies, and their health.

Chapter 7
A Faithful Companion

Animals are a gift from above for
they truly define the words, unconditional love.
–Heather Wolf

Pets were also a part of the American Revolutionary War. While their most common use was for hunting, dogs often played an important role for wartime soldiers as well, accompanying them while they were in combat.

They provided companionship and comfort to their owners, especially during the time they spent in the camps away from their loved ones.

Such is the case of the General of the Continental Army Division Charles Lee, who always liked to be accompanied by many dogs. This General was very fond of his pets and was known for this reason. Among his many companions, people remember him for his little dog named Spado.

The loyal and smiling little dog attracted a lot of attention and was his owner's favorite. In this story, we will tell you more about this peculiar pet and his relationship with his owner, General Charles Lee.

Historical Context

In 1775, when the Revolutionary War broke out, dogs were already part of the culture of the Thirteen Colonies established in the United States. However, in earlier years in Williamsburg, there was a law that prohibited any individual in the town from owning a dog.

Gradually, as science improved in the study and research on animals, it allowed people to have another perspective on dogs and other animals in which they considered the feelings and personalities of these individuals.

In 1776, *A Dissertation on the Duty of Mercy and the Sin of Cruelty to Brute Animals* was published by an Anglican clergyman named Humphrey Primate. The book was a document often referred to as the "Declaration of Independence for animals." Then, with the Enlightenment, came an acceptance of humane activities for animals, and the need for hunting dogs also spread.

By tradition, dogs herded livestock, carried messages, protected their owners, and carried packages. But the popularization of dogs as pets came sometime later. As early as the Revolutionary War era, it was common for soldiers to adopt stray dogs while on duty, both to carry messages, protect them from possible threats, and carry packages when needed.

General Lee and His Pets

Lee's deep attachment to his dogs, especially Spado, was well known. The man, who had a stubborn and restless nature, found it helpful to have the company of his pets to calm him down and find peace of mind in those troubled wartime days.

He found refuge in his animals, as they gave him the strength and energy he needed to recharge after a difficult battle. He had permission to travel with them so he always made sure that they received the best attention and had the necessary care in terms of food and hygiene.

Wherever Lee was going, they accompanied him; whether he was going to the hall, the garden, or the war camps. As we have to assume, Lee's loyalty and obedience were very important to his pets. He made sure to have them well-trained to be obedient to his master.

Training some of his dogs was more difficult for him than others, and in some cases, he was forced to use a leash to lead them. In Spado's case, he didn't need a leash; the puppy knew perfectly well what to do as soon as he heard his owner's voice. According to the signals Lee gave him, he went to him and obeyed his every command. The connection became so strong that they grew to understand each other very well.

It is speculated that Lee decided to adopt the animal from a trip he took to Portugal, where he quickly became attached to it.

General Lee had always liked strange names, so Spado fit very well with what he wanted; the meaning of the name being associated with a castrated animal or person. It was also an archaic term for a "sword or spade" from the 16th century in the Iberian Peninsula.

It wasn't just the name that made little Spado stand out, it was the little dog's personality that made him popular with Lee's friends and acquaintances. Spado would accompany him to some of the dinners organized by the General, and would be formally introduced to all the guests at the meeting.

Guests would make comments such as: "What a laughing dog he is, you can tell he is well trained," "How cute is his black color and unique coat? He does not go unnoticed," "I think Spado is a very particular dog. He generates a lot of interest."

Lee was nothing but proud about the compliments. He knew of Spado's great social skills and was confident that he would make a great impression on his acquaintances. The General made sure to give Spado the recognition he deserved since the small dog also helped him in the war camps with some tasks that would otherwise have been more burdensome for him. Let's just say it made his life in the army easier and more bearable.

A Singular Puppy

Spado, General Lee's little dog, was a Pomeranian, a breed of the Spitz type that is classified as a toy dog due to its small appearance. It is known to be very popular among royalty since the 18th century, an example of which is Queen Victoria, who owned a very small Pomeranian whose popularity became very immense.

Generally this type of dog weighs between 1.36 and 3.17 kilograms, and measures between 8 and 14 inches in height. With a robust form and a lot of fur, this little dog usually has a very feathered tail. They have a ruff of hair on their neck for which they are often known, and also have a fringe of feathery hair on their hindquarters.

As is the case with most Pomeranias, Spado was very friendly; not only with his owner, but the other dogs Lee owned. He was also very lively and full of energy to follow his owner in any of his exploits. Spado was very protective of his owner. Whenever he saw the general in danger, he would go out to help him in any way he could.

Spado was always alert to any external noise, the general had trained him for just that reason. This training helped Lee to be aware of the movements of the British soldiers.

Lee had trained him perfectly to be respectful with the rest of the group. Little Spado knew when and how he should act at a certain moment. Lee had socialized him from puppyhood so that he could tolerate the presence of other dogs, as well as strangers. Because of his size, a little supervision was always necessary to make sure he didn't have a mishap with another larger dog.

Spado and General Lee were very close, some would say they were thick as thieves. They needed each other and kept each other company.

An Unexpected Scare

Loss or Theft Announcement by the Virginia Gazette on March 7, 1777:

Wanted: A black wooly dog of the Pomeranian breed by the name of Spado. He belongs to the brave but unfortunate General Lee, and was seen at Wright's Ferry around the 25th of December.

You can imagine the anguish General Lee must have felt when he heard that the person, who he had commissioned to take Spado to Berkeley County because the general was busy, had lost him.

At that time, Lee had been accused of treason and it was feared that he would be deported to England. So he was busy with a series of paperwork and procedures, and entrusted his favorite dog to one of the men under his command.

The young man, whose last name was Block, was walking along some roads on his way to Berkeley County, which required crossing a river, when suddenly the little Pomeranian dog went astray.

In the days that followed, Lee was desperate. He contacted all of his friends and asked them about the dog. He moved land and sea to find him, and kept up to date with any news about Spado's whereabouts. Keep in mind that Spado was the dog of a Major General, who was George Washington's second in command, so what happened to him was going to be news anyway.

Luckily, Spado was found after a couple of weeks by a neighbor of the colony. According to her testimony, even though the dog looked hungry and a little skinnier than usual, he was in good spirits and energetic.

Lee could only shed tears of joy when he found out that Spado would be back home with him. Appreciative of what his neighbor did for him, Lee gave the reward offered to the lady who took care of him for a few hours and found him safe and sound.

Lee was very grateful to her, telling her, "You don't know how happy I am that you found Spado in good condition. I was very worried about him, and I thank you very much for seeing the ad and contacting me."

She replied, "You are welcome, General Charles Lee. It is such an honor for me to be able to help you in this simple task. I am grateful to you and your team for all you do for our country, and your continued fight. It's the least I could do for you."

A Quieter Life

Country life was always General Lee's preference; therefore, after the war ended, he devoted himself to a life as a planter, as well as writing occasionally for the *Maryland Journal*.

He had somewhat unusual habits in his way of life, but what prevailed above all was his love for animals. He had cows and was surrounded by many dogs, which he cared for with much affection and dedication.

Spado was no longer with him, but he always remembered him with great affection. He was grateful for all those years they had spent together in the war, for every camp and every victory they had celebrated together.

In his articles, he also included stories about his adventures with his pets and other animals, always emphasizing how meaningful their companionship was to him and what he had discovered about each pet he shared. Each one had a particular way of being, and he found this delightful. He was very interested in learning how to tame them or live with those that could not be tamed.

In his later years, he discovered that his greatest passion was his love for animals. Despite having been very proud of his war work and having absolutely no regrets about all his years of service, he had discovered another way of life that was very welcoming to him.

Lessons Learned

- From General Charles Lee, we can highlight his great affection and devotion for his pets, which he used to say were his best company and refuge in times of adversity. Sometimes four-legged animals give us a unique and very singular affection that other living beings do not give us. It is a different kind of affection, which is why many people choose to have a pet in their daily lives as a companion.

- As we can see in Spado's case, each dog has its own personality and characteristics. It is important to train them from an early age so they can relate better to their environment, just as human beings need a proper education to be able to coexist well with the rest of society.

- Although the loss of Spado was nothing more than a big scare for Lee, we could see how much he cared about his favorite pet and what he was capable of doing to keep him safe and sound. After all, he was part of his family, and his family was protected and cared for at all times.

- Although Lee held a very important position during the Revolution, it must be recognized that the rhythm of life for army soldiers is very hard. And it is logical to think that when they retire, they look for other calmer rhythms of life as this General did: dedicating himself to plantations and more domestic activities without leaving aside his most faithful companions–the puppies.

Chapter 8

Hancock's Distinctive Roles

*The growth and development of people are
the highest calling of leadership.*
–Harvey S. Firestone

John Hancock was a renowned Patriot of the Revolution, whose stylized signature on U.S. The Declaration of Independence was iconic to the point of being used in common American parlance to refer to someone who had to sign a contract.

This signature stood out for its legibility and also for its size. It was the one that stood out the most in this document of great transcendence for the American nation. People considered him one of the Founding Fathers of the United States since he played a very important role in the Revolutionary War, being the president of the Second Continental Congress and double Governor of the Commonwealth of Massachusetts.

Not only that, Hancock, having inherited a profitable mercantile business, decided to use much of his wealth to support the colonial cause amid the conflict between colonists and British soldiers.

An Elite Education

From a wealthy family, John Hancock was the son of a colonel. After the death of his father, he was sent to live with his aunt and uncle, Thomas and Lydia Hancock. The uncle was the owner of a company dedicated to commerce, known as the House of Hancock.

Both were very influential in shaping the character of John, who greatly admired the great business skills of his Uncle Thomas and the amiable temper of his Aunt Lydia. After high school, Hancock enrolled at Harvard College and received a B.A. degree in 1754, making his family proud.

At the outbreak of the war, the young man went to work for his uncle, from whom he gradually learned about the position and trained John to become a partner in the firm. As part of his work, he obtained great benefits, like receiving invitations to cultural events and a substantial salary that allowed him to afford certain luxuries, such as buying haute couture clothes.

Between 1760 and 1761, Hancock settled in England and then moved to Boston to work in the Hancock House when his uncle's health began to deteriorate. In August 1764, after his uncle eventually passed, John took over the business full-time.

Political Rise

Britain's debt after the Seven Years War influenced the British Parliament to try to tax the colonies with a series of acts that increased tensions between colonists and the British Crown.

The act also implied changes in the way trade was conducted to evade the measures imposed.

At that time, Hancock had become a well-known political figure. He was elected as a Boston city councilor; and although he initially maintained a moderate stance, when the Stamp Act came out in 1765, he joined the resistance by participating in a boycott of British products.

His stance only increased his popularity in the city of Boston, which resulted in his election to the Massachusetts House of Representatives in May 1766. His political success was also due in part to the support of Samuel Adams. Both supported each other to achieve their purposes and obtain more connections that would help them prosper in their respective fields.

Customs Incident

In time, Hancock became a more active member against British impositions. Even as part of his political activity, he snubbed the British authorities who invited him to attend events in the presence of customs officials.

There was an incident in which Hancock was accused of an illicit act involving the detention of a vessel named Liberty, which he owned. It turns out that one morning in May 1768, the small ship carrying a cargo of Madeira wine was inspected by customs workers when they noticed that it contained only a quarter of the cargo capacity.

The missing inventory raised the suspicions of the authorities, who thought that an unloading of more wine had been planned overnight so that taxes would not be paid on the full load. They consulted some sailors who were on the ship most of the night, but they claimed to have seen nothing.

One of them changed his tune after a month had passed, saying that he had been held on the vessel while it had been illegally unloaded. That was how Liberty was taken, which ended up causing a riot between Whigs (members of the British Liberal Party) and customs officials.

As a result of this altercation, the customs workers filed two lawsuits: one against the ship and the other against Hancock. At the end of the first trial, the plaintiffs and the royal officials ended up winning the lawsuit and keeping Liberty.

In a second trial, with John Adams as his attorney, the proceedings against Hancock were dropped and along with the charges against him.

The trial damaged Hancock's reputation and conflict among historians: some defending him and pointing out that he was the victim of a criminal blackmail scheme, and others accusing him of being a smuggler.

Several allege that the reason behind punishing him was for political reasons or to take advantage of the resources he possessed, and a series of speculations circulated in this regard. What is certain is that whatever it was, this incident undoubtedly remained in the memory of the Patriots and is part of revolutionary history.

Role in the Provincial Congress

Hancock was elected president of the Provincial Congress at a time when the country was in turmoil. The British Crown had repealed one of the so-called Coercive Acts to strengthen its control of the colonies, and the First Continental Congress had been created in Philadelphia to coordinate the measures to be taken by the American colonies in this regard.

During this time, Congress created the first companies of Minutemen, or militiamen from the colony who were prepared to go to war at any time.

In December 1774, the Provincial Congress appointed Hancock as a delegate to the Second Continental Congress. In turn, the Provincial Congress unanimously re-elected him as president in February of the following year. As we can see, the political figure of the Patriots was gaining strength, which allowed John to have legitimacy as a representative of Massachusetts.

There were rumors that Hancock could be imprisoned along with other Patriots, so he was advised to escape from the city of Lexington. However, he refused to leave at first, wanting to engage in combat. John Adams and his other companions convinced Hancock that it was not the best idea and that his role as a political leader came first.

In those days, the famous Battle of Lexington and Concord took place. And while Hancock fled, thousands of soldiers stayed behind and fought in the combat.

Role in the Presidency of the Continental Congress

Hancock succeeded Peyton Randolph as President of the Continental Congress in 1775. He was elected unanimously after Henry Middleton declined the nomination. He was the perfect candidate because he had experience assuming other offices of great importance in Massachusetts. Because he was born into a well-to-do social circle, he commanded respect and confidence from moderate delegates while his association with the Boston radical group made him easy for other radicals to accept.

During his tenure as Speaker of the House, Hancock performed the protocol activities of his office. In addition, he had to do some tedious administrative activities. The patriot was involved in an extensive controversy with Harvard, his alma mater.

There was some confusion over the return of some financial records and cash. Hancock had been Treasurer of the university before being elected by Congress to be president, but during that period, he could not bring himself to return the money. Therefore, they demanded that he do so through a public message.

This also brought him a series of problems with some of his political opponents and with his former university classmates.

Apart from some problems on a personal level, during this period Hancock had to deal with an extremely complicated political context. These complications all began in 1776 when Washington was expelled from New York City by the British, which caused Congress to move to Baltimore.

The situation of uncertainty continued in the following months, and they had to move around several places; Therefore, Hancock had to make decisions in a changing environment. He had to act as a sort of public relations consultant, constantly communicating with colonial officials on government business, as well as raising money and other supplies needed for Washington's army.

One of the most important events that took place during his administration was undoubtedly the Declaration of Independence. He put his signature on the document, which was large and extravagant. It caught everyone's attention and the phrase "sign your John Hancock" began to be used as part of the common American language.

Some rumors said that he did it deliberately so that the document could be read by any authority without the need for glasses. The truth is that we are not surprised by the extravagance of his signature, since it was true to his extroverted personality.

Last Years

Hancock returned to Boston and was re-elected to the House of Representatives. During this time, what stood out in his work was his philanthropic activity. Remember that after the Liberty Boat incident and Harvard's financial records, John's reputation and finances had been affected.

Despite this, Hancock was always very kind to his community. He made donations to the needy, visited widows and orphans, and when a friend needed him he always supported a friend when they were in need. His generosity added to his friendly character and made him a much-loved figure. People were grateful to him for the work he did in his political posts and his activism in the Patriotic struggle.

As we can guess, not everything was rosy for this Patriot. In the positions he held, Hancock had to face opposing officials who wanted to harm him, as well as the moments he missed with his wife and children, whom he missed very much.

He had to walk behind every movement he participated in since each procedure required time to be carried out effectively, such was the case when he joined other delegates from Massachusetts to sign the Articles of Confederation that were ratified only three years after having been requested.

In 1778, he wanted to lead men into combat. He commanded some 6,000 militiamen in the campaign, leaving the soldiers in charge of planning and delegating activities. Unfortunately, this did not go as planned. In the end, the so-called militia abandoned the plan. As expected, Hancock suffered some criticism for the disaster, but this did not greatly harm the popularity he had gained.

Still, despite not getting the results he expected, John felt good about himself because he had made his best effort, and it was something he had wanted to do for a long time. Also, added to all the good he had done for his people, this one setback in his career did not take a toll.

One of the most important offices he would hold until the end of the Revolutionary War was that of Governor of Massachusetts, which he won with 90 percent of the vote. Hancock, this time, maintained a much more peaceful position, avoiding controversial issues.

He stayed in office until January 1785, when his health issues forced him to retire. He spent his last years as acting governor. His farewell was something of a statewide festivity, his funeral being the largest of any given to an American to date.

Lessons Learned

- This patriot teaches us through his life story not to be afraid to face new challenges and to try. After all, even if we make mistakes in the process, it is worthwhile to strive for something we strongly believe in.

- Sometimes we will face people who want to harm us, and we must know how to take it calmly and act according to the situations we have to deal with. For example, in the case of Hancock's ship, fortunately, he had the support of his good friend John Adams as his lawyer. Likewise, he had the help of the people for the acts he had carried out in favor of the American people. So it is always good to have the support of those around us to confront people with bad intentions.

- Hancock was a man of great political trajectory. He assumed every position he held with great responsibility and knew how to solve problems following the advice of his closest friends and colleagues.

Chapter 9
Lydia's Power

Believe in yourself and there will come a day when others will have no choice but to believe in you. –Cynthia Kersey

L ydia Barrington Darragh is known as a heroine of the American Revolutionary War, where she participated in an act of Patriotism in which she saved part of General George Washington's militia from an attack by British troops.

Of Quaker origin (a religion whose worship is given primarily in silence and lifestyle is quite simple), this woman was born in Dublin, Ireland, and moved to Philadelphia at the age of 24 years old when she married William Darragh.

Her humanitarian background influenced her choice to work as a nurse and midwife for several years. Her generous nature and dedication to service contributed to Lydia's remarkably successful career.

As a result of her marriage to Darragh, Lydia became the mother of five children, the eldest of whom, Charles, would join the Continental Army. While raising her children with her husband, she also pursued her work, proving herself to be a multifaceted woman: exercising a role that was different from what a woman was supposed to be at that time.

Lydia and her husband lived a relatively quiet life. Part of their habits was to hold meetings in which they had long conversations about social reform causes. They were excellent hosts to their guests, and with them, they enjoyed some pleasant evenings.

Despite her religious background and quiet lifestyle, Lydia did not allow this to prevent her from acting in favor of the revolutionary cause when she had to. She became a spy to protect her country and her loved ones. Her determination and decisiveness enabled her to accomplish the feat that will be described in this story.

A Necessary Coincidence

Lydia Darragh was a housewife, caring for two of her children, when the British invaded Philadelphia in 1777. The militias of that country had decided to occupy some houses by force to use them as they pleased.

An example of this was the seizure of her neighbor's house, which was used as headquarters by a General named Howe.

You can imagine the anguish Lydia felt when she realized the danger she and her family were in. And worst of all, what she feared most came true: the day Major John André knocked on her door and ordered her to vacate her family home.

She kept her composure through it all and thought about going to Howe himself so that she could stay at home. She talked it over with her husband as well and they both decided it was for the best.

On the way, she met a British officer who happened to be her cousin, Captain Barrington, from Ireland.

"Cousin Lydia, how good to see you. What are you doing here?" Barrington asked her.

"Good to see you too, cousin. You don't know what has happened! There was a British soldier who came to see me, and he asked me to leave my home. I am living there with my husband and two of my children, and I have nowhere else to go! My two children are happily staying with relatives, but they will be returning soon. I ask you to please do what you can to let me stay," Lydia begged.

"Relax, Lydia. Rest assured, I will do my best to make sure that doesn't happen. I will talk to Howe and see what can be done," Barrington affirmed.

Barrington was a man of his word. Within a few hours, he had a conversation with General Howe, and Lydia was allowed to stay in her house on the condition that she keeps a room available for meetings between the soldiers and other senior British officers. Lydia agreed, and suddenly her house became a conference center for top British officers.

A Spy in Action

On the night of December 2nd, at Lydia's house, Howe's commanding officers were devising their plans for a major offensive that was approaching. Howe had spies to inform him of the Americans' next steps and knew they were at Whitemarsh, the site of the next attack.

Lydia had devised a hiding place from which she could listen intently to what was going on there: a linen closet adjoining the meeting room. Hours earlier she had already been notified by a British officer that a meeting was being scheduled for that very night, so the officers warned her and her family to go to bed early.

She already had a feeling that Howe and his men were up to something against the Continental Army; therefore, while they were meeting that night, she decided to get out of bed, grab her nightgown, and leave her room to her hiding place. From there, she got precise information about what they had concluded to do in that meeting. She immediately took notes, rolled up the paper on which she had written them, and kept them with her when she returned to her bedroom.

The Perfect Alibi

Evidently, after hearing what the British were planning, Lydia became concerned about her eldest son, Charles, who was in Whitemarsh. She had to act fast if she wanted to prevent the Americans in that city from the next attack.

She tossed and turned in all night, wondering what to do. The next morning she decided that she was the one who should carry the message directly. She came up with the following:

She asked her cousin for a pass to go and buy flour at a mill in Frank Ford on the outskirts of town. That did not arouse much suspicion since many humble people went to acquire goods in the countryside. There were also widows and single women who stayed home while their husbands were in the army. Going there meant crossing British lines, but as they were stapled goods that were allowed.

Lydia set out early one morning with an empty flour sack. She walked several miles through the snow, and ended up at a tavern by the name of Rising Sun. There she met a friend and companion of her son's, Thomas Craig. With luck, he had time to pass him some notes hidden in an old cloth needlebook, which contained the plans of the British.

The notes contained precise information regarding Howe's plans; they said that the general would leave with 5,000 men, 13 cannons, and 11 boats on wheels. Craig, upon receiving them, thanked her, and promised to take the information personally to General Washington's headquarters.

When the day of the attack on Whitemarsh arrived, the Americans realized that Washington's forces were already fully prepared to counterattack the British in the area. Howe noticed something strange, and they immediately suspected that information had been infiltrated.

The British spy chief reported the following:

"One thing that is very clear to me is that the enemy was already aware of our arrival. They were not taken by surprise and seemed well-prepared for us. There was nothing left for us but to fall back and desist in the offensive. Frankly, we felt outwitted and demanded an explanation."

It didn't take long for them to take action, and they called in some suspects upon their return to Philadelphia–including Lydia Darragh.

The Moment of "Truth"

Lydia was very clever and already knew what to say. She remained calm and collected, and when it was her turn to speak to the spy chief, she told him that she did not know about what had happened on the night of December 2nd. According to her testimony, all members of her family had gone to bed early that night when the officers met, just like they were told to do.

To Lydia's good fortune, he believed her; and although she left him with certain doubts about what had happened, Lydia's words were convincing. He told her:

"I know you are telling me the truth. That night, when I knocked on your door three times, you answered me the third time. It's unusual to me how the information could have leaked to General Washington. We must be more careful, because I suspect that the walls can talk."

That is how the housewife and midwife had played a trick on the great British spymaster, and he had completely fallen for it.

The great skills that this woman had to leak information and not raise major suspicions came to light with this feat. It is not just anyone's job to outwit an experienced espionage officer, but Lydia did it with great care and caution.

We must recognize something that also helped her was that Lydia publicly did not make her support for the revolutionary cause known, and that both she and her husband were known to be pacifists. All this contributed to her being the perfect candidate for a few more espionage actions on behalf of the Continental Army.

Her husband and children were very proud of Lydia's performance. She had learned how to deal with Army Officers and be convincing with her arguments. They would tell her things like:

"Mommy, we are very proud of you. For your creativity and skill in evading the suspicions of the British."

"Lydia, my beloved, what you did took a lot of courage for us and especially for the Patriot cause. You certainly showed a lot of guts in doing what you did."

"Mother, my companions and I thank you infinitely for risking yourself to save us. I will be eternally grateful to you."

Her life had taken a 180-degree turn, from midwife and housewife to a very skilled spy. Although she would not dedicate herself to it for long, her contribution was well recognized in the years to come.

Later Years

Much was questioned as to whether the work of women spies in the Revolutionary War was valued. The officers did not usually mention their presence in the documents or narrate in detail how significant their contribution was in leaking information.

The truth is that in many other cases, Lydia Darragh's work was slow to be appreciated and valued by scholars and recognized institutions. In 2013, this would change. The National Society for the Sons of the American Revolution created the Lydia Darragh Medal. This medal recognized the assistance of women who worked behind the scenes supporting SAR programs.

Upon her husband's death in 1783, Lydia continued to raise the couple's children while working in a clothing store. As always, she kept a positive attitude and liked to spend time with her loved ones, who were a great support system for her. She recalled, from time to time, those anecdotes with fondness and pride.

Lessons Learned

- Lydia's case shows us the multiple facets in which a woman can perform. With time, we have come to realize the determination of some women, such as Lydia, to take on roles that at the time were seen as exclusively male activities. Characters like Lydia break through those walls and are good examples of women who fight for their country, who have their voice, and who are the main drivers of their destiny.

- We should not underestimate ourselves if we want to try a new facet due to lack of experience. Lydia managed to fool a well-known spy chief, she gave him false testimony without hesitation, and it worked. Just because someone is more qualified or experienced does not mean we cannot have the same skills as that person to fill a particular position or role.

- It is always good to ask for help when you need it, Lydia did this with her cousin when she met him by chance so she could stay in his home, and this allowed them to stay there for a long time.

Chapter 10
A Four-Legged Hero

Talent wins' games, but teamwork
and intelligence win championships.
–Michael Jordan

W e seem to underestimate the value of horses in the history of American independence. For they are not given much consideration when it comes to the celebrations on the 4th of July of each year, nor are they often mentioned in texts about this event.

However, the role they played was extremely important. We have been able to verify this with some facts that have been mentioned throughout this book.

We have been learning how the horses helped some of the heroes of the Patriot cause to arrive in time to warn of a possible British ambush, and how they helped them move from one place to another while they were fighting in combat.

Horses accompanied soldiers, who had to fulfill an order at the last minute, on long and tedious journeys. They also accompanied the American soldiers during some very significant events during the fight for American independence. Surely you have heard of Paul Revere and his famous midnight ride on April 18, 1775; or you might remember the first story in this book, which spoke about Sybil Ludington–a girl who showed her incredible riding skills one early morning in the rain and the middle of a lush forest.

These feats were made possible precisely because of the skills of both: the riders and their horses. While it is true that one of the main functions of these animals was to transport soldiers, they were also used to patrol and move weapons and supplies. They also pulled cannons, roads, and wagons of all kinds.

In addition, the physical appearance of war horses gave soldiers courage by increasing their morale and helping them to intimidate their opponents during battles. With them by their side, the efficiency of the soldiers increased, and they had more resources to think about their next moves.

In the case of the horses of one of the most well-known figures of this war were named Blueskin and Nelson. We can say that they served as an inspiration to Commander George Washington to improve his skills as a horseman and focus on reinforcing the skills of the members of his infantry.

Let's say that war horses enhanced the image of the Independence rebels. It is enough to imagine Washington mounted on his horse, leading his battles with great fanfare to get excited and perceive his personality as a knight and brave officer.

The attitudes of the Patriots won them the respect of their British opponents, who were surprised and pleasantly impressed by the leaders of the American Revolution.

The Other Heroes of the American Revolution

One of the first cavalry units used in the Revolutionary War was that of Captain John Leary of the Light Horse Troop. This company consisted of about 40 light dragoons. In 1775, they were accepted as a Continental unit.

To have a greater advantage in achieving small victories, the men of the troops used the so-called "reconnaissance." This is a process in which a military unit watches a determined area in search of the enemy. Thanks to this action, the cavalrymen were able to recognize the British soldiers (who were distinguished by their red coats) from miles away and, thus, were able to plan their next moves in the battle.

At a key moment in the war, when the so-called "redcoats" were becoming aware that they were at a disadvantage, George Washington ordered cavalrymen to patrol the Atlantic coastline and pass on the coordinates of British troop movements if they were seen coming by sea.

Washington's troops included a total of 260 cavalrymen. These men were important in preventing the British from advancing and making use of their supplies as the continental cavalry units planned an ambush to take away the hay they would use for their infantry. As a result, they left the "redcoats" defenseless and unable to move anywhere.

This is an example of the opportunities that the Patriots of the American Revolution gained against the great British Army through the use of cavalry troops. Speed in moving, transporting heavy supplies, and planning the occasional ambush are some of the advantages obtained thanks to these animals of great endurance and strength.

A Skilled Horseman

Stories abound of George Washington being a successful horseman, it is common to find several famous images showing the American Commander leaping across roads in a hurry to reach his destination.

Another usual image of the leader was encouraging his countrymen to enlist on the battlefield. It was as if the horses gave him the power to face even the most fearsome of his adversaries.

Proof of this is the narrative that mentions Washington, with his battle-hardened Virginia soldiers amid a great battle, where he vehemently asked them not to back down from fighting against the British Army. He told them not to be afraid of the British and to stand up for their country.

The Commander is described as capering on horseback before several of the Pennsylvanians as he exclaimed, "Parade with me, my brave fellows! There's only a handful of enemies, and we'll have them straight." (Mount Vernon Ladies Association, 2023)

Blueskin and Nelson

Major General George Washington is known to have had two main mounts during the Revolutionary War. One was a gray, Arabian horse by the name of Blueskin. This was a very special companion for Washington since it was a gift from Colonel Benjamin Tasker. With a white coat, this horse became very popular in the artistic representations of this famous Patriot.

The other horse that kept Blueskin company was named Nelson. This animal was more docile and easygoing than his companion. Both were very important and valuable assets in the battles the Patriots faced. They had been well trained by Washington to perform as hard as the other horses in his army.

Blueskin was a one-of-a-kind horse to Washington as his Arabian lineage allowed him to have a lot of stamina, be able to endure very long journeys, and be on the move for a great deal of time. Of course, like any other animal, he also had his weaknesses. He was very prone to get upset by loud noises; so, according to the circumstances, Washington decided whether it would be best to take him or Nelson.

Of course, when he was very exhausted, he was left to rest so that he could recover. Blueskin was a horse that attracted a lot of attention because of his white coat and black skin, which made him look bluish in the sunlight.

Because of his less gentle character, Blueskin did not accompany Washington to several battles like Nelson, but he did participate in several important battles. Both Blueskin and Nelson followed their owner's orders, and each performed different roles in the Revolutionary War.

A Very Special Bond

Fortunately, both horses managed to resist the vicissitudes of the war, but others did not have the same luck. It should be noted that for American officers taking care of their troops also meant taking care of their cavalry, as they were a crucial part of defining a possible victory.

Without them, they would not have been able to make long journeys to warn their comrades of what was happening on the battlefield and send them medicines or other much-needed supplies.

Several accounts highlight the great concern of Washington and other members of the Continental Army to care for these little animals. They also point out that the connection with them was such that they felt that both rider and horse cared for each other. It was like a protective instinct that arose between the two that made them aware of each other during the long days they faced together.

For the riders it was of vital importance to control their horses in adverse situations such as a fight under fire, they had to know well the personality of the horse they owned and how to make them obey them when everything around them was in chaos.

The Importance of Good Preparation

Any experienced rider is aware that knowing how to control a horse is more a matter of understanding the animal's temperament and fears than trying to force them to do an activity they are not quite ready for. Let's just say that by force, they were not going to achieve anything and could end up pushing the animal away.

War horses have to be well-trained before going into battle. The rider must make sure that the horse can stop if he hears a gunshot or a loud noise, as these can trigger the animal to run away or bolt.

Being herd animals by instinct, they tend to imitate other horses; so if they see a fleeing action, they can replicate it. For the same reason, it is advisable to reinforce their mental strength and courage. Although some horses are indeed predisposed to have a calm personality, the most important thing when selecting a horse for war is that they have adequate training so that they are ready to face these panic situations.

This can be done using an exercise where a battle is simulated, and these animals learn to adapt to it. In the 18th century, some horses used to stand in front of a line of cannons to acclimatize to fire. The charisma of the trainer is also important because not everyone can read the animal and understand its emotions and tensions.

In Washington's case, for example, it is said that the horses often approached him with joy when he visited them. The people around him noticed the great enthusiasm with which he prepared them for their fights: always exceeding the expectations generated.

Blueskin's Retirement

Both horses were discharged after the War. In the case of Blueskin, he was transferred to Mount Vernon, and after that, he was returned to his original owner, Colonel Benjamin's wife.

Of course, the horse had suffered from his use during the Revolutionary War. As was to be expected, he showed signs of aging and significant physical wear and tear. However, Mrs. Dulany,the Colonel's wife, accepted him with much love and affection. She was willing to take care of him in his last years and treat him with the utmost care. She knew handling Blueskin required time and dedication, but she loved him very much as he had been her youthful horse and great companion. She was truly happy to have him back by her side.

Besides, she saw his seemingly worn appearance as a symbol of all the hard work he had done during the Revolutionary War. As a Patriot, and having witnessed firsthand some of the most important events of the war, she was very proud of Blueskin.

The bond between them became stronger as the days passed. They enjoyed sunny walks in nature and spent time at home resting with the rest of the family.

Lessons Learned

- As we can see, horses are animals with unique characteristics that made them very resistant and strong when participating in the combats like the ones of the American Revolution. We must also take into account that they required a lot of care and good preparation before soldiers took them to battle.

- The control that the owners exercised over the horses in the Revolutionary War era depended largely on how well they knew them, so it was necessary to spend time with them and decipher which tools worked best with each personality type so they would perform well in battle.

- In the case of Blueskin and Nelson, both were different horses not only in the breed but also in skills and abilities, so Washington required both of them for different occasions.

- It was a joint effort that both riders and horses performed on the battlefield: both needed each other and fought in duplicity to represent the Patriot side during the American Revolution. They could not have done it without each other, which is why these animals should get more recognition during the celebration of Independence Day.

Conclusion

Stories that Inspire

As we have already mentioned at the beginning of the book, the purpose of these ten stories is to describe and reflect on the characters who played different roles in the struggle for American independence.

In this conflictive time that was the Revolutionary War: it was the Patriots and rebels,who remained firm in their position to achieve the long-awaited freedom. We learned the story of an African-American man named James Forten, who decided to stay on a British ship as a prisoner of war rather than take the opportunity to go to the opposing side; thus demonstrating his loyalty to his country and his shipmates.

We also met a very talented horsewoman by the name of Sybil, whose bravery allowed her neighbors and family to stay safe from possible attacks by British soldiers. The young woman ventured on a long journey through muddy trails to gather her father's men so that they could safeguard the safety of their village.

We were amazed by the story of Deborah Sampson, who dressed as a man to be part of the Continental Army and fight for her country. We also discovered Lucy Knox, who, from her role as a housewife and with her great festive spirit, was a very important emotional and moral support for her husband Henry, who spent most of this time in the war camps during the outbreak of the American Revolution.

All this left us with great lessons, such as the importance of keeping in touch with our loved ones in difficult times and being faithful to our convictions despite the temptations that may come our way. We learned that youth or lack of experience does not impede facing our fears and moving toward what we want to achieve.

Have you ever wondered how these characters were able to have such guts and be able to perform the actions they did?

Well, I'll tell you a secret, we all have different abilities that come to light as we go through the different stages of life. You, who are still very young, have a whole world to discover. I assure you that you are stronger and braver than you think, and you don't need to be part of a war, as was the case of these characters, to discover it.

The Patriots or great heroes of the American Revolution did not act alone. Perhaps in the most famous books, only a few are mentioned, but there are more people involved in the success of this great struggle for the Americans. George Washington would not have been able to face the hardest battles without his great companions, Blueskin and Nelson. They were horses with different characteristics, but equally important to their owners.

It is necessary to know how to value those who were part of our history to understand that everything we have today did not happen overnight, and that obtaining the independence of the United States, in this case, was a process of constant struggle.

From the 18th century to 2023, there are more than two centuries of difference, and it is worth asking ourselves how much we have changed as a society. What acts of these heroes would we like to see replicated through our rulers? How much more work needs to be done to achieve a just and equal society?

These are questions I want you to put down on paper to serve as an invitation for future research into the most representative events of our history. Doing so will allow you not only to obtain more culture and topics of conversation, but also to learn from the mistakes and successes of these characters.

We must also emphasize recognizing the work of the other heroes of this Revolutionary War. We must give them the value they deserve and understand that their homeland owes them deep gratitude for their work. We should not belittle any role and should be proud of all these Patriots who, with their efforts, built the nation that now makes up the United States of America.

May their deeds fill us with motivation to take a leap into the past, refresh our memories, and remember that we are here to build a more just and healthy world.

Without further ado, I would like to point out that some parts of the book have fictitious accounts to adapt these stories in a war context to a children's audience and maintain a tone suitable for the youngest members of the household.

References

American Battlefields Trust. (2021, March 25). *American dogs.* https://www.battlefields.org/learn/articles/american-dogs

American Battlefields Trust. (2023). *Joseph Plumb Martin: Voice of the common American soldier.* https://www.battlefields.org/learn/articles/joseph-plumb-martin

American Battlefields Trust. (2023). *Lucy Flucker Knox.* https://www.battlefields.org/learn/biographies/lucy-flucker-knox

American Battlefields Trust. (2023). *Lydia Barrington Darragh.* https://www.battlefields.org/learn/biographies/lydia-barrington-darragh

American Battlefields Trust. (2023). *Sybil Ludington.* https://www.battlefields.org/learn/biographies/sybil-ludington

Anirudh. (2020, February 26). *10 major effects of the American Revolution.* https://learnodo-newtonic.com/american-revolution-effects

Barkley, Charles. (2016). *Charles Barkley's black history month all stars: All star #7: James Forten.* https://thephiladelphiacitizen.org/james-forten-facts/

Boozman, John. (2016, March 16). *Deborah Sampson's legacy.* https://www.boozman.senate.gov/public/index. cfm/2020/3/deborah-sampson-s-legacy

Commonwealth of Massachusetts. (2023). *Deborah Sampson: American Revolutionary War hero.* https://www.mass.gov/ info-details/deborah-sampson-american-revolutionary-war-hero

Duray, Sammie. (2017, July 4). *The horses that led us to independence.* https://www.theplaidhorse.com/2017/07/04/the-horses-that-led-us-to-independence/

Encyclopedia.com. (2019). *Joseph Plumb Martin.* https://www. encyclopedia.com/history/educational-magazines/ martin-joseph-plumb

Fandom. (n.d.). *Dogs in the American Revolutionary War.* https:// military-history.fandom.com/wiki/Dogs_in_the_ American_Revolutionary_War

Gilder Lehrman Collection #: GLC06046. (2009-2023). *Forten, James (1766-1842) Letters from a man of color, on a late bill before The Senate of Pennsylvania.* https://www.gilderlehrman.org/ collection/glc06046

Greer, Jason. (2023). *When travelers rest was the American frontier: The story of "Dicey" Langston Springfield.* https:// travelersresthere.com/2017/05/27/travelers-rest-american-frontier-story-dicey-langston-springfield/

Hagist, Don N. (2018, August 2). *War horses gone astray.* https:// allthingsliberty.com/2018/08/war-horses-gone-astray/

Hatmaker, Julia. (2018, October 5). *James Forten is a Pennsylvania Patriot you didn't learn about in history class (but should have).*

https://www.pennlive.com/life/2018/10/james_forten_
was_a_freedom_fig.html

History is Now, Magazine. (2019, October 6). *Joseph Plumb Martin
and the American Revolution: Yankee doodle dandy.* http://
www.historyisnowmagazine.com/blog/2019/10/6/
joseph-martin-plumb-and-the-american-revolution-
yankee-doodle-dandy

Hoehling, A.A. (1993). *Women who spied.* Madison Books.
https://books.google.es/books?hl=es&lr=&id
=Tjt5CfcOJXEC&oi=fnd&pg=PP1&dq=lydia+
darragh&ots=it-YTO0gO5&sig=sSXQ-oyZ3O-
456U2bfMAFn3Gqow#v=onepage&q=lydia%20
darragh&f=false

Infogalactic: the planetary knowledge core. (2016, January 13).
Deborah Sampson. https://infogalactic.com/info/Deborah_
Sampson

Junior Scholastic. (2019, September 2). *Girl Hero of the
American Revolution.* https://junior.scholastic.com/
issues/2019-20/090219/girl-hero-of-the-american-
revolution.html#960L

Kiddle Encyclopedia. (2022, August 7). *Dogs in the American
Revolutionary War facts for kids.* https://kids.kiddle.co/
Dogs_in_the_American_Revolutionary_War

Klein, Christopher. (2021, September 30). *The Midnight Ride of
William Dawes.* https://www.history.com/news/the-
midnight-ride-of-william-dawes

Martin, Joseph Plumb. (1995, January 1). *Yankee Doodle Boy: A
young soldier's adventures in the American Revolution as told
by himself.* Holiday House. https://bookshop.org/p/

books/yankee-doodle-boy-a-young-soldier-s-adventures-in-the-american-revolution-joseph-plumb-martin/9810598

Mount Vernon Ladies Association. (2023). *Equestrian in war.* https://www.mountvernon.org/george-washington/farming/the-animals-on-george-washingtons-farm/horses/equestrian-at-war/

Museum of the American Revolution. (2013, July 16). *Memoir of a Revolutionary Soldier.* https://www.amrevmuseum.org/read-the-revolution/memoir-of-a-revolutionary-soldier

Museum of the American Revolution. (2018). *Meet Joseph Plumb Martin–Performance.* https://www.amrevmuseum.org/meet-joseph-plumb-martin-performance

National Park Service. (2021, November 27). *Joseph Plumb Martin.* https://www.nps.gov/people/joseph-plumb-martin.htm

Peterson, Vivienne, (2009, March). *Pomeranian Project.* https://www.germanspitzandpomeranianproject.org/story-of-spado

Prillman, Sonali. (2021, March 1). *The Revolutionary War heroine Sybil Ludington.* https://www.historicamerica.org/journal/2021/2/28/csek71aqux7oh1iq1vt9522bjqepsb

Revolutionary War. (2020, March 4). *Dicey Langston.* https://www.revolutionary-war.net/dicey-langston/

Revolutionary War. (2020, March 4). *Lydia Darragh: Quaker, pacifist, and American spy.* https://www.revolutionary-war.net/lydia-darragh/

Serfilippi, Jessie. (2023). *Deborah Sampson.* https://www.mountvernon.org/library/digitalhistory/digital-encyclopedia/article/deborah-sampson/

The American Revolution Institute of the Society of Cincinnati. (2023). *Engraving of Charles Lee with his Dog.* https://www.americanrevolutioninstitute.org/asset/engraving-of-charles-lee-with-his-dog/

The Constitutional Walking Tour. (2020, June 30). *James Forten–One of America's Founding Fathers.* https://www.theconstitutional.com/blog/2020/06/30/james-forten-one-americas-founding-fathers

The Editors of Encyclopaedia Britannica. (2022, December 13). *Deborah Sampson, United States soldier.* https://www.britannica.com/biography/Deborah-Sampson

The Editors of Encyclopaedia Britannica. (2023, January 8). *John Hancock.* United States statesman. https://www.britannica.com/biography/John-Hancock

Tikkanen, Amy. (2023, January 1). *Lydia Barrington Darragh.* American war heroine. https://www.britannica.com/biography/Lydia-Barrington-Darragh

Tomes, Luke. (2021, January 14). *6 Key Causes of the American Revolution.* https://www.historyhit.com/causes-of-american-revolution/

Trive in Grade Five. (2020). *Lucy Flucker Knox.* https://thriveingradefive.com/american-revolution-stories-for-your-students/

Trive in Grade Five. (2020). *Sybil Ludington.* https://thriveingradefive.com/american-revolution-stories-for-your-students/

Ushistory.org. (1995, July 4). *Signers of the Declaration of Independence.* https://www.ushistory.org/declaration/signers/hancock.html

Wallace, Willard M. (2022, December 4). *American Revolution.* United States history. https://www.britannica.com/event/American-Revolution

Wallenfeldt, Jeff. (2022, December 4). *Sybil Ludington American Revolutionary War heroine.* https://www.britannica.com/biography/Sybil-Ludington

Warren, Jack D., Jr. (2020, February 20). *Joseph Plumb Martin, Everyman.* https://www.americanrevolutioninstitute.org › Blo...

Watson, Elwood. (2007, January 17). *James Forten (1766-1842).* https://www.blackpast.org/african-american-history/forten-james-1766-1842/

Wikipedia, the free enciclopédia. (2022, July 31). *Pomeranian dog.* https://en.wikipedia.org/wiki/Pomeranian_dog

Wikipedia, the free enciclopédia. (2022, August 20). *Lucy Flucker Knox.* https://en.wikipedia.org/wiki/Lucy_Flucker_Knox

Wikipedia, the free enciclopédia. (2022, August 27). *List of Patriots (American Revolution).* https://en.wikipedia.org/wiki/List_of_Patriots_(American_Revolution)

Wikipedia, the free enciclopédia. (2022, September 28). *Blueskin (horse).* https://en.wikipedia.org/wiki/Blueskin_(horse)

Wikipedia, the free enciclopédia. (2022, November 21). *Dogs in the American Revolutionary War.* https://en.wikipedia.org/wiki/Dogs_in_the_American_Revolutionary_War

Wikipedia, the free enciclopédia. (2023, January 11). *Joseph Plumb Martin.* https://en.wikipedia.org/wiki/Joseph_Plumb_Martin

Wikipedia, the free enciclopédia. (2023, January 20). *Lydia Darragh*. https://en.wikipedia.org/wiki/Lydia_Darragh

Wikipedia, the free enciclopédia. (2023, January 25). *John Hancock*. https://en.wikipedia.org/wiki/John_Hancock

Women History Blog. (2010). *Famous Spies, Women in the American revolution - Lydia Darrag*. https://www.womenhistoryblog.com/2010/09/lydia-darragh.html

Women History Blog. (2023). *Dicey Langston, South Carolina Revolutionary War Patriot*. https://www.womenhistoryblog.com/2009/04/dicey-langston-springfield.html

Women History Blog. (2023, January 19). *Lucy Knox, Wife Of Revolutionary War Patriot Henry Knox*. https://www.womenhistoryblog.com/2009/04/lucy-flucker-knox.html

Wood, Paul A. (2022, February 18). *Laodicea "Dicey" Langston Springfield: South Carolina Revolutionary War Heroine*. https://www.southcarolina250.com/wp-content/uploads/Dicey-Langston-09-29-22-Interactive.pdf

Yardley, Alfredo. (2023). *SS4H4: The students will explain the causes, events and the results of the American Revolution*. https://slideplayer.com/slide/3560476/

Made in the USA
Las Vegas, NV
25 October 2023

79650801R00066